MUSEUM OF LONDON

PREHISTORIC LONDON

Nick Merriman

London: HMSO

CREDITS

Copyright in the illustrations lies with the Museum of London except for the following:

Satellite image of the London area (inside front cover), *National Remote Sensing Centre*; the Dagenham idol (p 1), *Colchester & Essex Museum*; tundra landscape (p 8) and glacial spring meltwater (p 8), *GeoScience Features Picture Library*; reconstruction of *Homo erectus* woman (p 11), *Commonwealth Institute*; Swanscombe skull (p 11), *Natural History Museum*; Trafalgar Square 120,000 years ago (p 14), *Illustrated London News*; painting of Neanderthals (p 14), *Giovanni Caselli*; Staines enclosure (p 22), *Fairey Air Surveys*; Stanwell cursus (p 22) and Wimbledon Common hillfort (p 36), *Aerofilms Ltd*; excavations at Runnymede (p 23 & 31), *The British Museum*; Mayfield Farm enclosure (p 31), *G K Thomas*; excavations at Uphall Camp, Ilford (p 41) and Moor Hall Farm, Rainham (p 45), *Passmore Edwards Museum*; Shepperton Neolithic complex (p 24) and Late Bronze Age axe from Shepperton Ranges (p 34), *Surrey Archaeological Unit*.

The following objects are from the collections of the British Museum (those asterisked have replicas on display in the Museum of London):

King's Cross Road handaxe (p 12), Petters hoard (p 33), Chertsey shield (p 38), Waterloo helmet* (p 42), Hounslow boar figures (p 42), Battersea shield* (p 47).

Photographs: Torla Evans, Richard Stroud, Trevor Hurst, Jan Scrivener.

Illustrations: Lyn D Brooks Associates, Frank Gardiner, Derek Lucas, Alan Sorrell.

I would like to thank the many colleagues who have generously provided information for this book, and commented on earlier drafts.

CONTENTS

© Copyright of the Board of Governors of the Museum of London 1990
First published 1990

ISBN 0 11 290447 5

British Library Cataloging in Publication Data
A CIP catalogue record for this book is available from the British Library

Printed in the United Kingdom for HMSO
Dd 292002 C100 9/90

Thinking About Prehistory

The word 'prehistory' covers any time before written records. Writing was developed at different times in different parts of the world, but in Britain it first became widespread after the Roman invasion of AD 43. Although 'prehistory' can cover any time as far back as the origin of the Earth, this book examines the period between the arrival of humans and their ancestors in the London area and the coming of the Romans.

The main way in which we find out about this period is through archaeological fieldwork. In Greater London there are very few areas of countryside where scatters of artefacts in fields might reveal sites or where aerial photographs may be taken, so the main method of investigation is excavation. The location of prehistoric sites is very difficult to predict, and in many of the cases noted in this book, prehistoric material has been discovered in the course of excavations designed principally to find out about later periods. After excavation, analysis of the site involves the study of structures, finds and evidence such as pollen from plants. Each plant has its own distinctive pollen, and

Clockfaces. *Representing the prehistoric and modern timescale in terms of a twelve-hour day.*

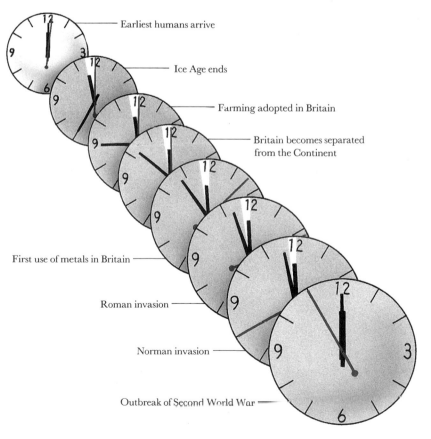

Earliest humans arrive

Ice Age ends

Farming adopted in Britain

Britain becomes separated from the Continent

First use of metals in Britain

Roman invasion

Norman invasion

Outbreak of Second World War

the microscopic study of these grains can tell us what the environment was like at different times. A range of scientific methods can help to date archaeological finds. In the first part of the book most of the dates come from the dating of deep-sea cores by a technique known as oxygen isotope analysis, and the later ones come mainly from the radiocarbon method, and have been corrected to give calendar years. Much of the evidence that is found is open to a number of different interpretations, and these are continually changing as new discoveries are made and new ways of thinking about the evidence are developed. What is presented here, then, is just the story that is thought to be the most accurate one so far.

It is difficult for us to understand how massive the prehistoric timescale is, and how huge the changes are that have occurred during it. Planet Earth formed approximately 4,600 million years ago, with life beginning about 600 million years later, and dinosaurs walking the earth between 225 and 65 million years ago. In comparison, our first human ancestors emerged only a few million years ago, in Africa, and their descendants did not reach the London area until about half a million years ago, when this book begins. For almost all of prehistory they lived by gathering plants, nuts and fruit, or by hunting, fishing or scavenging for their food. Farming was only developed about 6,000 years ago in Britain, and the Romans invaded just less than 2,000 years ago. Even when it is only concerned with the time humans have been in the London area, the prehistoric period is immensely long: it covers about 400,000 years, or 20,000 generations (great-great-great-great plus 19,996 great-grandparents!). In comparison, the Roman invasion was only 100 generations ago, and the Norman Conquest only about 50 generations ago.

Although this book is about 'Prehistoric London', London of course did not exist as a place until the Roman period. Until then, the area now covered by urban sprawl was simply part of the Thames valley. In areas such as Oxfordshire, aerial photography has shown that the valley was quite densely occupied at various stages of prehistory, and excavation in Greater London is now beginning to show the same density of occupation.

The London Basin

Beneath London's roads, buildings and archaeological deposits, is the underlying geology of the London Basin, which has always influenced the pattern of human settlement.

The London Basin is a depression which is drained by the River Thames, from the Goring Gap near Reading to the sea. It is roughly triangular in shape, with a point in the west by the Berkshire and Hampshire Downs, widening out to the east, bounded by the Chiltern Hills and the East Anglian Heights to the north, and the North Downs to the south. The rivers cutting through these chalk hills, such as the Colne, the Lea and the Roding in the north, and the Wey, the Mole and the Darent in the south, are the main drainage features of the basin apart from the Thames itself.

The story of the formation of the London Basin begins when all of Britain was covered by sea around 70 million years ago. This sea laid down chalky mud made of the skeletons of dead microscopic algae. The basin was formed as a depression where this mud settled down to form a layer of up to 150 m (500 ft) thick over the site of the shrunken sea. Then, a layer of sands and gravels was laid down on top of this about 60 million years ago, and about five million years later the London Clay (through which the London Underground is cut) was laid down by a deep sea which covered the London area

(*Right*) The main phases of London's prehistory.

500,000 BC	River Thames flows through Vale of St. Albans Advance of ice sheets down to north London Thames deflected into its present valley Earliest human presence in London area
400,000	Occupation at Swanscombe
300,000	Succession of cold and warm phases, during which three Thames terraces are formed Human occupation known through hand-axes found in gravels
200,000	Warm phase (130-110,000 BC) during which there are elephants and hippopotami in the London area. Britain separated from the Continent
100,000	Last glacial period: lower sea level, land bridge exposed. Probable occupation by Neanderthal people, who are replaced around 28,000 BC by Homo sapiens. Gradual thaw from 13,000 BC

10,000 BC	Sea levels gradually rise
	Change from tundra conditions to forest of birch and pine
8,000	Hunters of reindeer and wild horse along Colne Valley
	Mixed forest of lime, oak and elm. Change to exploitation of forest resources. Occupation of West Heath site, Hampstead
6,000	Britain separated from the Continent
	Farming adopted in Britain; permanent villages and fields; pottery-making
4,000	Occupation of Neolithic sites at Staines and Runnymede
	Cursus monument built in Stanwell area Metalworking introduced into Britain
2,000	Cremation cemeteries; aurochs burial in west London Dividing-up of the landscape

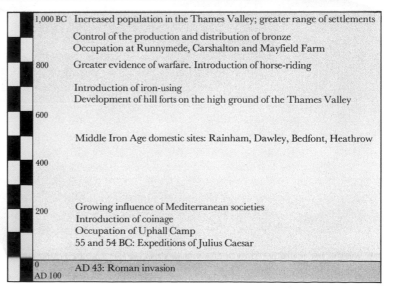

1,000 BC	Increased population in the Thames Valley; greater range of settlements
	Control of the production and distribution of bronze Occupation at Runnymede, Carshalton and Mayfield Farm
800	Greater evidence of warfare. Introduction of horse-riding
	Introduction of iron-using Development of hill forts on the high ground of the Thames Valley
600	
	Middle Iron Age domestic sites: Rainham, Dawley, Bedfont, Heathrow
400	
200	Growing influence of Mediterranean societies Introduction of coinage Occupation of Uphall Camp 55 and 54 BC: Expeditions of Julius Caesar
0 AD 100	AD 43: Roman invasion

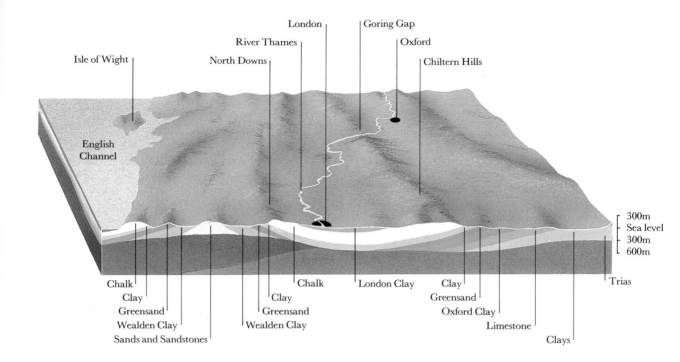

Isle of Wight

English
Channel

North Downs

River Thames

London

Goring Gap

Oxford

Chiltern Hills

300m
Sea level
300m
600m

Chalk
Clay
Greensand
Wealden Clay
Sands and Sandstones

Chalk
Clay
Greensand
Wealden Clay

London Clay

Clay
Greensand
Oxford Clay
Limestone

Trias

Clays

The London Basin. *An idealised cross-section.*

and the North Sea. It varies from 4.5 m (15 ft) thick in west London to over 150 m (500 ft) in east London. Finally, in certain areas such as north-west Surrey, Hampstead and Highgate, are layers of fine-grained 'Bagshot Sands'. To all of these 'solid' deposits have to be added the 'superficial' or 'drift' deposits which were laid down, relatively recently in geological terms, during the Ice Age. These include boulder clay and gravels in north London marking the furthest southerly extent of the ice-sheet, a series of river gravel terraces running along the Thames and its tributaries, and the 'brickearth' soil which caps them in many places.

In cross-section the London Basin is bowl-shaped, with the oldest deposits sloping upwards to appear at the edge of the bowl, and the most recent deposits in the centre. This occurs because of the way in which the basin was formed, and because the erosion of the chalk hills to the south has exposed the older deposits. As a result, it is a varied landscape, and the type of deposits at the surface in any particular area have had an important effect on human settlement of the region.

Throughout prehistory the London Basin provided first an excellent environ-ment for hunters and gatherers, with a range of foods such as nuts, berries, birds, animals and fish to exploit, and later on an ideal farming environment. In addition, it offered plenty of resources such as timber, clay, flint and iron. In the later prehistoric period the chalk hills were settled, possibly for sheep farming, and were the site of defended settlements with commanding views over the valley. The heavy London clay lowlands which reach the surface in north-west London, south-east Essex, south London and north Kent, would generally have been forested for much of prehistory, but would nevertheless have been exploited for timber and supported specialist settlements, for

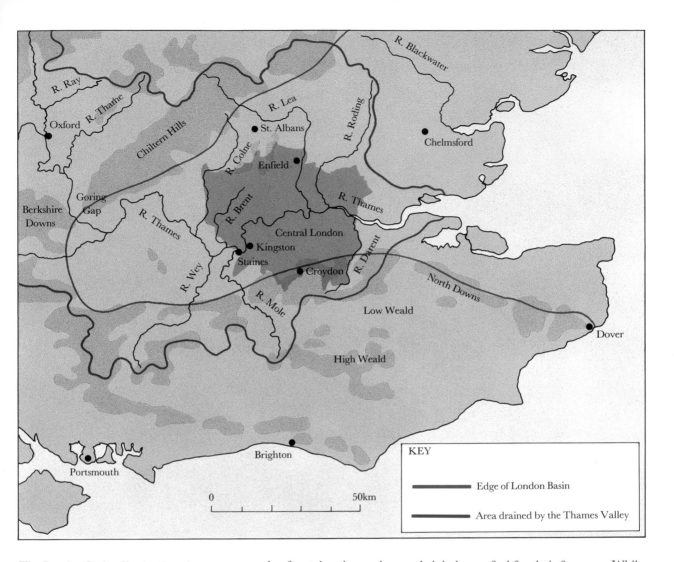

The London Basin. *Showing the main landscape features.*

example of metalworkers, who needed timber as fuel for their furnaces. While many of the sands and gravels overlying the London clay probably had a low agricultural value, the river gravels and their brickearth capping were relatively fertile and intensively settled throughout the prehistoric period. Even the marshy deposits of river mud known as alluvium were exploited as pastures at various periods. The Thames and its tributaries also provided an excellent communication route connecting Britain with northern Europe. Some of these rivers have almost entirely disappeared from view now, having been clogged by mud and rubbish, diverted, embanked, or channelled into drains. In central London for example, some of the lost or nearly-lost rivers include the Westbourne (which provides water for the Serpentine in Hyde Park), the Tyburn (which flows into Westminster), the Fleet and the Walbrook (in the City of London), and the Effra, the Peck and the Neckinger (which flow through Southwark and Lambeth).

THE HUNTERS OF THE ICE AGE

Introduction

Over 2 million years ago, for reasons still not fully known, the Earth experienced a gradual cooling, so that temperatures dropped to around five degrees centigrade lower than they are today. Even this slight shift was enough to ensure that more snow fell in the polar regions and mountains than melted in the summer. The end result was that in Britain, from at least half a million years ago, the ice-sheets advanced slowly from the north and reached down as far as the London area at their greatest extent.

However, the term 'Ice Age' is rather misleading because, over this half-a-million-year period, temperatures varied greatly, and were sometimes as warm as today, or warmer. The term, then, is a general name for a period during which there was an alternate cycle of cooler and warmer periods, each lasting tens of thousands of years. For most of the time conditions were in fact just slightly colder than today, and the London area looked like the Russian steppe or Norwegian tundra. Winters would generally have been harder than now, but snow would have melted in the spring to reveal plants attractive to animals. In Britain, significant ice advances occurred around 450,000 years ago, and this was followed by at least two main cycles of warmer and then colder periods until the final disappearance of the glaciers around 10,000 years ago. At the moment, it is not certain whether the Ice Age has come to a natural end, whether we are in a temporary warm period which will eventually turn cold, or whether human interference in the climate will result in a further global warming.

(Below) Tundra landscape. *A modern photograph taken in Greenland showing the relative lushness of tundra in springtime.*

The Great Freeze and the Diversion of the Thames
(500,000–440,000 BC)

500,000	400,000	300,000	200,000	100,000	BC/AD

(Left) The edge of a glacier. *A modern photograph from Italy showing conditions at the edge of the ice sheet similar to those in north London around 450,000 BC.*

The first people arrived in Britain about half a million years ago when the climate was relatively mild. For most of the Ice Age, Britain was joined to the continent where the English Channel now is, so people could simply walk across to Britain, following game animals as they migrated. At this time, the River Thames actually flowed through the Vale of St Albans to East Anglia, and may have joined the Rhine in a large delta in what is now the southern North Sea. This meant that not only could people walk across from the Continent, they could walk along a corridor of land without having to cross any major rivers. The earliest Palaeolithic (Old Stone Age) sites found so far are in Sussex, Somerset and Suffolk, so it is probable that the migrants passed through the London area. However, no remains definitely dating to this period have yet been found there.

As the climate gradually cooled, the ice sheets expanded further and further south. At the period of maximum glaciation, around 450,000 BC, they were

(Right) Britain in the Ice Age. *The map shows the land bridge joining southern Britain and France. The Thames is shown first following its original course through the Vale of St Albans and then its modern course when it was pushed into its present valley by the advance of the ice sheets.*

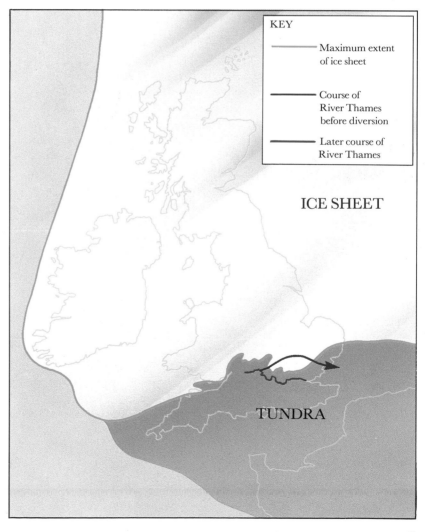

KEY

——— Maximum extent of ice sheet

——— Course of River Thames before diversion

——— Later course of River Thames

ICE SHEET

TUNDRA

up to 330 m (1,000 ft) thick, and reached down as far south as Finchley and Upminster in the future area of London. The rest of London would have been permanently frozen ground, and further south into France would have been tundra. The sea level would have been at least 100 m (330 ft) lower than today, but it was probably so cold that no game animals, and no humans, lived in this bleak peninsula of Europe.

The crucial event as far as the story of London is concerned is that during this great glacial period the weight of the ice sheets creeping down from the north blocked the river and forced it southwards out of its old valley in the Vale of St Albans, and realigned it from near Uxbridge into the valley it has occupied ever since. The presence of the river Thames is the main influence on the prehistoric settlement of the London region, so our story really begins with this event.

The Earliest Human Presence (440,000–297,000 BC)

| 500,000 | 400,000 | 300,000 | 200,000 | 100,000 | BC/AD |

As this great cold period came to a close and the climate became warmer, people recolonised Britain and we have the first definite evidence for human activity in the London area itself. The earliest humans to enter the area were members of the species *Homo erectus* ('upright man'). They walked on two legs and made tools, and seem to have been the first hominids to spread out of Africa. Although none of their skeletal remains have been found in the area, large numbers of

(*Left*) Handaxes. *These two flint handaxes from Swanscombe were chipped from natural nodules of flint. The whitish 'cortex' surviving on the lower example is the surface of the original nodule.*

(*Below left*) Swanscombe. *Reconstructed scene around 350,000 years ago. Collecting plant food was probably as important as hunting. All members of the social group would have participated actively in gathering and hunting.*

(*Right*) Homo erectus. *Reconstruction of a female* Homo erectus, *around 400,000 BC.*

(*Below*) The Swanscombe skull. *The three conjoining fragments of the skull were found on three separate occasions in 1935, 1936 and 1955. Together they form the oldest human remains yet found in Britain.*

the flint tools they used for chopping up meat and plants have been found. Probably the oldest flint tools in London have been found in Hillingdon in the gravel of one of the river terraces formed during this period (see p. 12). These tools are known as 'handaxes', probably a multi-purpose cutting and chopping tool used for digging up roots, cutting wood and preparing food.

One of the most famous sites where such tools (although slightly later in date) have been found is at Swanscombe, a gravel quarry by the Thames in north Kent. The site consists of several layers representing successive periods of time, and containing different kinds of stone tools. Animals found in the early levels of the site include straight-tusked elephant, rhinoceros, wild ox, wolf, bear, boar, duck and pike, some of which may have been caught or scavenged by these early inhabitants, who chopped up the carcasses with the stone tools.

Over a period of nearly 150,000 years the climate fluctuated sharply, sometimes being as warm as today, usually being slightly colder. During this long period, people gradually evolved from *Homo erectus* to a new species, *Homo sapiens* ('wise man'), to which we all belong. The oldest human remains in Britain in fact come from the Swanscombe site. They consist of three parts of the rear section of a skull which seems to have belonged to a male aged about twenty-five and, in evolutionary terms, the skull shares characteristics with *Homo erectus* and *Homo sapiens neanderthalensis* ('Neanderthal man'). Its dating is not quite certain, but may be over a quarter of a million years old. The site also has some of the earliest evidence of fire in Britain, which may have been started naturally, or used deliberately to stampede game animals such as horse or giant ox into traps or ambushes. As well as eating meat, people living in rough shelters by the banks of the Thames a few hundred thousand years

ago would have collected plant food such as fruit and nuts. They probably would have been hairier than people are now, but as the climate was often considerably colder than that of today, they would certainly also have needed the protection of some sort of clothing to survive. This would no doubt have been made from the furs and skins of the animals they hunted or scavenged.

Shaping the Landscape (297,000–130,000 BC)

500,000	400,000	300,000	200,000	100,000	BC/AD

Around 300,000 years ago, the climate cooled again and another glacial period began. This time it lasted for 167,000 years and contained several alternating cold and warm periods within it. One of the main legacies of this period is a series of river terraces which still underlie the London region. Their presence can be felt, for example, at Trafalgar Square where there is a rise in ground level at the junction of two terraces.

These terraces were formed as the climate became increasingly cold with the onset of glacial conditions. More and more water became trapped on land in the form of ice in the north of Britain. The weight of this ice caused northern Britain to sink and southern Britain to rise slightly. At the same time, there was more water in the Thames, which cut a much deeper channel to reach the sea. Over thousands of years, the cutting of this deeper channel left the former floodplain of the river high and dry. Once the river had cut its new course it formed another floodplain, eroding its banks and depositing large amounts of sand and gravel carried down by the meltwater.

Then, very slowly, as the climate began to enter a warmer phase, the force of the river slowed down and it began to meander. Gradually it settled to a main channel and vegetation grew over the flooplain rather like it does today outside the built-up areas. Finally, when another colder phase started,

(*Below*) Handaxe from near the King's Cross Road. *Up until the 17th century AD, these implements were thought to be 'fairy arrows' or bolts of lightning. This example found with mammoth bones, helped to show they were ancient human artefacts.*

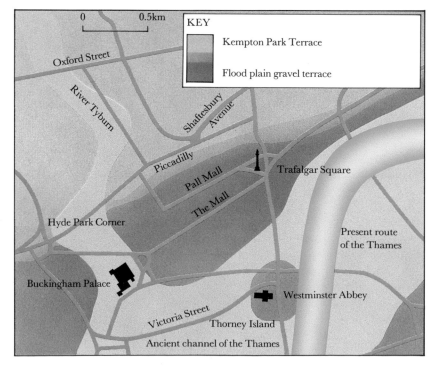

(*Left*) Terraces around Trafalgar Square.

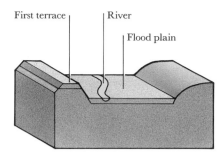

First terrace | River
Flood plain

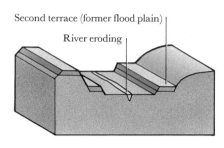

Second terrace (former flood plain)
River eroding

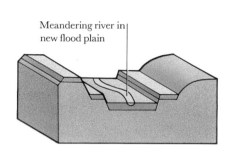

Meandering river in new flood plain

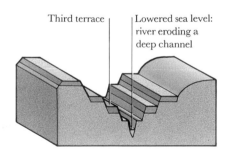

Third terrace | Lowered sea level: river eroding a deep channel

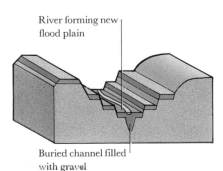

River forming new flood plain

Buried channel filled with gravel

Formation of River Terraces.

the process began to repeat itself, with a deeper channel being cut to reach the lowered sea level and the previous floodplain being left as a terrace.

At least six of these terraces have been identified in the Thames valley in the London area. The oldest, known as the Black Park terrace, which can be seen at Hillingdon in west London, was formed after the Thames had been deflected southwards out of the Vale of St Albans. The next three, known respectively as the Boyn Hill, Lynch Hill and Taplow terraces, were formed between 297,000 and 130,000 BC, and the final two, the Kempton Park and Floodplain terraces, were formed during the final cold period 110,000 – 10,000 years ago. These terraces, especially the Lynch Hill terrace, contain the great majority of the earliest human artefacts known from the London region. Most of them, however, are not in their original position, having been moved by the force of the glacial river. One of the first objects to be recognised as a prehistoric handaxe was found in about 1690 near the Kings Cross Road. At the time it was found with the bones of 'an elephant', which was almost certainly a mammoth. As people then only thought the world was about 5700 years old, they looked for references to elephants in Classical literature, and concluded that the axe was a spearhead thrown by a native Ancient Briton at a war elephant of the Emperor Claudius's invading Roman army in AD 43.

Often flint tools were moved by river action and left in concentrations, but sometimes they have not been displaced very far and occur as spreads of material. One of the most famous of these sites is at Stoke Newington in north-east London, where a great many handaxes were found towards the end of the last century during the building of the houses which now cover the area. The site also produced wood and plant remains, including two artificially-pointed birch stakes (unfortunately no longer preserved), but the dating of these is not certain. In other parts of London, such as West Drayton or Yiewsley in Hillingdon, hundreds of handaxes have been found in the course of gravel extraction, especially in the last century when this was done by hand rather than by machine.

Elephants in Trafalgar Square: The Last Interglacial Period (130,000–110,000 BC)

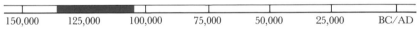

| 150,000 | 125,000 | 100,000 | 75,000 | 50,000 | 25,000 | BC/AD |

After the long cold phase, the average temperature slowly increased until it was a few degrees warmer than that of today, and the sea level slightly higher. Probably for the first time, the land bridge to the Continent was flooded by the rising waters of the North Sea, and Britain was cut off from the Continent. Possibly because large areas of the country were covered with an impenetrable forest, so far there is no sign of human activity in Britain in this period. There is evidence, however, that the London area was occupied by animals such as the elephant and hippopotamus, which we nowadays associate with much warmer climates further south. The Trafalgar Square area, right in the busy heart of modern London, has been the main site of these animal findings.

Elephant remains from Pall Mall and St James's Square were first reported in 1758 and over the last 200 years many more finds have been made and carefully recorded when new buildings were erected around Trafalgar Square.

In the late 1950s excavations in the area revealed the bones of elephants, hippopotami, rhinoceroses, wild oxen, red deer, fallow deer and lions. The ground conditions had also resulted in the preservation of small insects and the pollen and seeds of nearby plants. The insects included dung beetle, cockchafers, weevils and water beetles, and the pollen included that of grasses, hazel, maple, hawthorn, and water chestnut.

This evidence has enabled scientists to show that at the time the Thames was swiftly flowing with a great deal of weed. The river's edge where the hippopotami wallowed would have been marshy and surrounded by rushes, while the countryside behind was fairly open grassland.

The Last Glacial Period (110,000–13,000 BC)

150,000	125,000	100,000	75,000	50,000	25,000	BC/AD

Very gradually the temperature cooled and a forest of spruce and pine developed, between about 100,000 BC and 50,000 BC. During this time, Neanderthals were occupying Europe, probably having evolved from *Homo erectus*.

Flint axes from Hillingdon. *These kind of axes, used in the hand or mounted in a haft, may have been used by Neanderthal people visiting the London area in the early part of the last glacial period.*

(*Left*) Glacial landscape. *This reconstruction shows the kind of landscape encountered by Neanderthal hunters in northern Europe.*

Although no physical remains of Neanderthal people have been found in the London area, a few flint tools thought to have been used by them have been found, for example at Sipson Lane in Hillingdon, west London, where a handaxe was excavated by a Museum of London team. Even these finds, however, are few and far between, and it seems that southern Britain was an inhospitable outpost of Europe at this time. It probably only supported a small population of migratory hunters who walked across the land bridge from the continent, which was again exposed by the lowered sea level. One possible example of the work of these hunters was found during the nineteenth century in Southall in west London. An apparently complete mammoth skeleton, with numerous stone tools around it, was found by workmen digging a trench. One of these tools was a flint spearpoint described as actually touching the bones. It is of a type which probably dates to this period, and many more examples have been found in excavations in the Ealing/Acton area, especially around Creffield Road where recent excavations have been conducted. Unfortunately, nothing survives of the mammoth today, so we must wait for further discoveries.

Apart from a warmer period between about 41,000 and 36,000 BC, the climate was a cold one, and the environment was a grass-sedge tundra, with scattered willow, juniper and dwarf birch shrubs. At this time the principal animals were mammoth, woolly rhinoceros, wild horse, reindeer and giant deer. During the full glacial, lasting from about 26,000–13,000 BC, glaciers again covered northern Britain and the sea level was at least 100 m (330 ft) lower than that of today. It was at about this time that the deposits of soil known as 'brickearth', which has supplied much of the material for London's brick buildings were laid down, partly from windblown dust from the river floodplains of meltwaters further north. It was also during this period that the two lowest Thames terraces were formed, together with the Buried Channel. This was formed when the sea level was particularly low and the river

(*Below*) Mammoth kill. *A speculative reconstruction showing how a mammoth might have been hunted by separating it from the herd and driving it onto boggy ground.*

had to cut a very deep channel, which eventually became filled with gravel when the sea level rose again. The river bed was never cut so deeply again, and as a result the old Buried Channel lies as a series of gravel-filled hollows deep beneath the present bed of the Thames.

One extremely important event occurring in this period is the replacement of Neanderthals by *Homo sapiens sapiens*, who was anatomically the same as us, but had very different customs and beliefs. On the Continent this occurred some time around 40,000 BC, but in Britain, stone tools normally associated with modern people do not occur until at least 28,000 BC. In the London area, a small number of flints from around this period suggest that some hunters were following herds there on their seasonal migrations. As mammoth and rhinoceros bones have been found in the Buried Channel during excavations for tunnels, it is likely that any evidence for human occupation at the time when the channel was flowing is also buried deep within it.

(Right) Butchery site. *Excavations at Uxbridge revealed scatters of bones of reindeer and wild horse, together with the flint tools used to butcher them.*

The Thaw and Recolonisation (13,000–7000 BC)

150,000	125,000	100,000	75,000	50,000	25,000	BC/AD

Finally, conditions began to warm up again around 13,000 BC and the sea slowly rose, reaching about 40 metres (132 ft) below its present level around 8,300 BC. During this time the environment changed from being a treeless steppe-tundra to one of birch and pine. Most importantly, there is more definite evidence for colonisation by groups of people who simply walked across the land bridge from the continent. The country may not have been entirely empty, but it is probable that Britain has been continuously – rather than seasonally – occupied from at least this period.

(Below) Uxbridge, 10,000 years ago. *This reconstruction, based on recent excavations, shows reindeer migrating northwards along the valley of the River Colne in the area of present-day Uxbridge.*

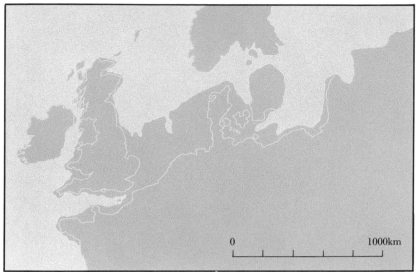

(*Right*) Britain *c.* 8000 BC. *The land-bridge to the continent is still exposed as the sea level is lower, and some areas now covered by the North Sea are dry land.*

(*Above*) Refitting flint core and blades. *The Uxbridge excavations produced long flint blades and cores of the Late Glacial period. Some, such as the blade on the right, showed evidence of wear where they had been used to work antler. Many blades could be fitted back onto the cores from which they had been struck.*

In this environment the new colonists found few big game such as mammoth left (they died out in around 10,000 BC). Instead they had to concentrate on hunting reindeer and wild horse. Two of their temporary encampments have been excavated by a Museum of London team in the valley of the river Colne in west London. The earliest, dating to about 8000 BC, consisted of a scatter of blade tools made of flint, interspersed with reindeer and horse bones, while another, perhaps some 2,000 years later, was a group of slightly different flint tools and bones of red deer. Many of the long flint blades can actually be refitted onto the cores from which they were struck, showing that tools were being made, used, and then discarded on site. It seems as though each scatter represents one particular occasion when the hunters were butchering their prey by the river before transporting the meat joints to their more permanent camps.

The birch forest rapidly spread, and as the climate warmed it was followed by a forest of pine and hazel, together with a heath of grasses, sedges, crowberry, and juniper bushes. Although Britain was still joined to the continent, formerly dry areas of the North Sea were now marshy and areas of higher ground, such as Dogger Bank, were covered in pine forests and perhaps inhabited by bands of hunter-gatherers. The Thames and the Rhine joined up to drain into the English Channel. Along the Thames itself, fishing would have been an important source of food, perhaps as important as meat from the forest animals, and there was probably a seasonal pattern of fishing, fowling, trapping, hunting and gathering plant food. Except at Uxbridge, little of the evidence for this sort of activity has survived, although there is the exciting possibility that some early sites may still be preserved in deep mud in the Thames, because the river level has risen substantially since this period. An intriguing insight into what may still survive came recently from a deposit excavated at Peninsular House in the City of London, which was shown by pollen analysis to represent the remains of a marshy depression. In about 7500 BC it was surrounded by willows, and had sedges and grasses growing nearby, together with wild flowers such a buttercups, marsh marigolds, meadowsweet and mint. Even now, small patches of surviving material can tell us a huge amount about this distant period, and it is certain that our views will change greatly over the coming years as more discoveries are made.

The Wildwood and the Forest Hunters (7000 BC–4500 BC)

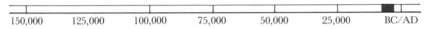

150,000	125,000	100,000	75,000	50,000	25,000	BC/AD

By about 7000 BC the London area was covered with a mixed forest of lime, oak and elm, with scatters of pine, birch and hazel. This dense forest supported a range of animals quite different from those living in the previous colder and more open landscape. These included red deer, elk, and the wild cow or aurochs, and they were difficult to track and hunt because of the dense vegetation. Accordingly, people had to change their hunting tactics in the same way as, generations before, people further south in Europe had had to change theirs as the forest spread. They domesticated the dog to help them in finding prey, and adopted the bow and arrow to kill animals at a distance. Using flint axes they also occasionally chopped down trees to create clearings in the forest where new shoots would attract animals to feed, and used fire to flush animals out of their hiding places. Possible evidence for this has been found at the Uxbridge site, where a layer above the scatter of flints and bone has been interpreted as the remains of a sedge marsh which had been extensively burnt.

At around this time Britain was finally separated from the continent by the rising sea. There may also have been a rise in population density as coastal and riverside areas became flooded and people moved inland. As a result, we can see that most areas in the London region became exploited: characteristic Mesolithic (Middle Stone Age) finds have been made all over the sandy hills and heathlands as well as in the valleys, which continued to be the main focus of occupation. The later scatter of flints and red deer bones at Uxbridge dates to this period and probably represents a small campsite, similar to ones which have also been found under the peat in the valley of the River Lea at Broxbourne in Hertfordshire.

(*Above*) Hampstead Heath, 8,000 years ago. *An imaginary reconstruction of a band of hunters stalking red deer in a clearing in the natural 'wildwood' around the area now covered by Hampstead Heath.*

(*Right*) Microliths. *These tiny flint implements were excavated from a site at West Heath, Hampstead. They would have formed parts of larger tools and weapons.*

(*Below*) Antler digging tools. *These mattocks were probably used for grubbing up roots and digging post holes for shelters.*

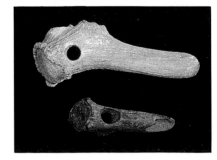

In this more enclosed landscape, it may not have been as necessary to follow migrating animals as it had been in previous times. In some areas it might have been possible, by taking advantage of a wide range of food resources, to live almost permanently in one small territory.

A hunting camp dating to around this period has been excavated on Hampstead Heath in north London. After an early phase of occupation in a more open landscape, which was subsequently abandoned, a small camp was set up near a stream. The excavators found the remains of several camp-fire hearths and thousands of flint tools. These included projectile points for hunting, 'scrapers' for removing flesh from animal hides, sharp blades used for cutting, 'gravers' for scoring bone and leather, piercers for making holes in leather, and the 'microliths' which are characteristic of this period. These are tiny flints carefully struck and flaked, often into geometric shapes, which seem to have been used as basic elements in a kit for making tools and weapons such as saws or arrowheads. Additional finds from the Thames show that antler- and bone-working was highly developed.

As in the earliest periods, fishing and fowling is likely to have been very important, and this time there is a certain amount of evidence for it in the form of barbed bone harpoons or fish-spears from the Thames, and from arrows that may have been used for hunting birds. At the Uxbridge site, favourable conditions even preserved bones of birds and fish which may have been caught by the occupants. Travel in this marshy landscape would have been mainly by canoes, fashioned from skins or hollowed out from tree-trunks using the flint axes and adzes that came into use for the first time during this period. Hundreds of these axes have been found on numerous sites in the London area and especially in the Thames.

The gravel islands or 'eyots' that protruded from the surrounding marsh in the Thames would have been ideal places to camp while fishing or setting traps for birds, rather as Fenlanders did in East Anglia before the Fens were drained. Few of these are now recognisable as islands, except in the west (Chiswick Eyot, Eel Pie Island), though some of them survived into medieval times, being distinguished by the name-ending '-ea' or '-ey' meaning 'island'. Examples include Chelsea, Battersea, Thorney (Westminster), Bermondsey and another at Southwark.

(Above) Axe, arrow and fish spear. *The axe, in a modern shaft, was used for felling trees for timber. The arrow, also in a modern shaft, is made from two small flint flakes secured to the shaft with resin. The fish spear would also have been mounted on a long shaft.*

FARMERS AND TRADERS

The First Farmers and the Last Hunters (4500–3700 BC)

| 5000 | 4000 | 3000 | 2000 | 1000 | BC/AD |

Probably the greatest change in British society before the Industrial Revolution came just over 6,000 years ago. This was when, after nearly half a million years of hunting animals and gathering wild plants, people started deliberately to plant and cultivate crops, domesticate animals and live in permanent villages. The reasons for the adoption of this Neolithic (New Stone Age) way of life are unclear, but increased population was undoubtedly a factor. Even though it is harder work than hunting, in the long run farming allowed a greater number of mouths to be fed. Increased population meant that farmers could dominate nearby hunters, who might eventually have adopted farming themselves. With permanent settlements, greater numbers of people, and the need for food storage over winter, a more hierarchical society grew up.

(*Above*) Wheat and sickle. *Experimentally re-grown emmer wheat originally deriving from the Near East, with a flint sickle (in a modern handle) used in harvesting the grain. It was found in the Thames, opposite the Tate Gallery.*

Clearing the wildwood. *The earliest farming communities probably hacked new fields from the forest during the autumn after the harvest. Each year they would have expanded the clearance away from their settlement, leaving the tree stumps in place until they rotted and sowing the seed amongst them.*

(*Above*) Stone axes. *These axes, one in a modern haft, were dredged from the Thames. As well as being important in clearing the wildwood, they also served as symbols of authority and may have been deposited in the river as offerings. The left-hand one is made of stone from Cornwall; the other two are polished flint.*

(*Below*) Neolithic sheep and goat. *The earliest domesticated animals differed little from their wild counterparts.*

In parts of Britain and Ireland, the cultivation of crops such as wheat and barley seems to have begun around 4500 BC. The crops and domesticated animals used are not native to Britain and so they must have been imported. It is not certain, however, whether large numbers of settlers brought them over from the Continent and displaced the native hunter-gatherers, or whether the natives traded the new crops and animals and adopted the new way of life. Probably a mixture of both occurred.

The earliest indication of the change towards farming in the London area comes from evidence preserved in a sample of pollen from near the West Heath site, Hampstead, dating to around 3800 BC. This shows that the tree cover had been disturbed, allowing grassland plants such as mugwort to grow, as well as some cereals. Probably this is the beginning of the clearance of the 'wildwood' to make small fields.

Within a few hundred years, using a combination of fire, stone axes and musclepower, people made a great impact on the landscape, clearing large areas for fields which they would hoe by hand to plant the cereals. Cattle and pigs probably browsed in the forest or on meadows near the river. The new way of life was not universally adopted at the same time, however, and hunting and gathering groups probably continued to live on in forested areas for many generations.

Another indication of a Neolithic lifestyle is the adoption of pottery vessels for cooking and storage. The earliest pottery bowl from inner London, perhaps as much as 6000 years old, was excavated in 1981 from a site in Clapham. Apart from this, little evidence for the very earliest phase of farming has been found in London. On the higher gravel terraces there are few signs of occupation until around 3000 BC; the earliest occupation found so far is on the floodplain of the Thames at sites such as Runnymede (3900–3600 BC) and Staines. Either farming was adopted at a fairly late date in the London area because the native hunter-gatherers felt less pressure to change, or the evidence is yet to be found. The latter is more likely, because the river around 4500 BC would still have been up to 5 m lower than that of today, so the very early sites may still be buried beneath deep silt deposited when the river levels rose.

Certain aspects of the life of the early farmers were little different from those of the previous hunter societies. Transport, for example, still relied to a large extent on the waterways of the Thames and the nearby creeks and marshes. No boat survives from this period, though there is a tantalising nineteenth-century reference to a canoe made of a hollowed-out tree trunk, with a stone axe lying in the bottom, which was found in Erith marshes. People still wore clothes made of hides, and there were no animals for ploughing, although they may have been used to pull carts by this time. The range of tools remained basically the same, with the exception of one new tool which symbolises the great changes that occurred. This is the stone axe, used to chop down the primeval forest and clear small fields for cultivation. As well as being used for this purpose, the axe seems to have been regarded as a symbol of power or authority, and highly prized polished axes made of rare stone were exchanged over great distances. As in all of prehistory, religion affected all areas of people's lives, from the times they planted crops to the way they made their tools. The River Thames seems to have had a ritual significance from at least this period. So many fine stone axes have been found in the river that they were probably thrown in deliberately as offerings rather than lost in accidents. The idea of 'Old Father Thames' seems very ancient indeed.

Settled Villages and Ritual Landscapes (3700–2200 BC)

By the early fourth millennium BC, a pattern of cleared fields, meadows and settlements was gradually beginning to emerge in the landscape of the lower Thames. Once farming was adopted, people's lives would have revolved around the cycle of preparing the fields, planting, tending and harvesting. The first fields would have been small clearings hacked out of the forest and hoed by hand amongst the fallen tree trunks. Over many generations, more and more fields were cleared until a farmed landscape appeared, with oxen being used to break up the ground with an ard (an early plough) by perhaps 2500 BC. People probably lived in large family groups in small clusters of huts near their fields, fairly isolated from other communities.

The two most informative sites of this period lie opposite each other on the Thames just outside London, at Staines and Runnymede. The Staines site, known as a 'causewayed enclosure' because it consisted of two concentric rings of interrupted ditches, was excavated in the early 1960s. With a maximum diameter of over 150 m (500 ft), it encloses an area of 2.2 hectares (5.5 acres). Some evidence of domestic occupation was found, but the site probably also served as a large meeting-place for seasonal bartering, marriages, celebrations and rituals, rather like a medieval fair. Long-distance exchange is attested by fragments of axes made from stone which comes from North Wales and the Lake District, and evidence of rituals is found in the form of parts of two human skulls, together with a forearm and a lower jaw, which were found in a ditch. In 1989, traces were found of a similar site just across the river

(*Above*) Staines causewayed enclosure. *This aerial photograph shows the Neolithic site as two concentric interrupted circles, before excavation.*

(Above) Neolithic houses. *Careful excavation on the site of Runnymede showed the presence of rectangular houses from the lines of rubbish that had accumulated against their outside walls.*

(Right) Neolithic flintwork. *All of these pieces were excavated from the causewayed enclosures at Staines. They include an arrowhead, knives, scrapers for preparing hides, and an awl for piercing leather.*

(Left) Stanwell cursus. *The long double-ditched feature running from bottom right to top left was thought to be a Roman road until excavation showed it to be over 3,000 years earlier.*

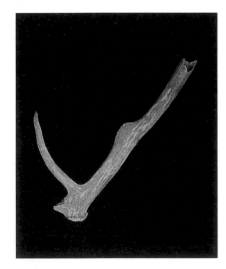

(Above) Antler pick. *Tools such as this one found in the Thames were used to dig the ditches of settlements and ritual monuments.*

(Left) Cursus reconstruction. *The cursus is shown crossing the river Colne in the area just to the north west of the modern Heathrow airport. In the right-hand corner is a contemporary ceremonial enclosure.*

at Runnymede, with remains of the earliest Neolithic houses known in the London area. These consist of rectangular buildings, probably with walls of wattle and daub (interlaced branches plastered over with lime and dung). Lines of broken pottery and flints were found along the outside of the buildings where they had accumulated as rubbish against the walls, and lines of stake holes showed internal room divisions. An insight into the diet of the period is provided by some of the pottery from Runnymede, which contained residues of honey, pork dripping and fish. The presence of honey is particularly interesting as it suggests possible management of bees at this early date, with their honey being used as a sweetener and in drinks such as mead.

Other evidence of settlement at this early period around 3000 BC is difficult to find. An unusual structure was excavated in 1963 in Rainham, east London, consisting of a circular ditch 15.25 m (50 ft) in diameter with a pit in the middle, both containing pottery and flints of this period, but its purpose is unknown. Otherwise, only occasional pits and scatters of flint suggest where the settlements of these early farmers might have been.

In the next phase, the early part of the third millennium BC (3000–2500 BC), the best-preserved monuments so far discovered were probably related to the religious beliefs of the farming societies of the London area. By far the most impressive is an avenue of two parallel ditches 22 m (77 ft) apart (probably with flanking banks) which run for at least 4 km (2.5 miles) from under the western edge of Heathrow Airport at Stanwell, across the River Colne and the River Wraysbury, ending just before the Bigley Ditch. Little is known about the function of these remarkable constructions, known as 'cursus' monuments, but they were almost certainly connected with religious rituals, perhaps based on the sun or moon. A similar but smaller cursus excavated at Springfield in Essex had a circular wooden structure at one end. Half a mile away from the Stanwell cursus, now under Runway 1 at Heathrow

Airport, a small interrupted ditch enclosure was excavated in 1969. No firm dating evidence was found, so the structure remained unexplained until a similar one was excavated three miles to the south on Shepperton Green by the Surrey Archaeological Unit in 1989. This consisted of a similar interrupted ring ditch with an initial phase which included a female torso and a more complete male skeleton placed in the ditch, and then a later phase with large amounts of decorated pottery, some antlers, and an abundant amount of struck flint. Outside the ring ditch a thick deposit of rubbish was found associated with a square pit probably used for boiling meat, and a long series of postholes marking out what may have been a path leading from near the enclosure to the adjacent River Ash. The function of these monuments is not at all clear, but it is possible that they were connected with ancestor worship. It is interesting to speculate that this small enclosure is not unlike a causewayed enclosure in layout, and that, as human bones were found at the sites at Staines, Runnymede and Shepperton, they may be related in some way with different aspects of funeral rituals connected with ancestor worship.

Pottery, already manufactured from around 4500 BC, was initially quite plain, but by about 3300 BC, highly decorated wares were produced and many vessels seem to have been highly-prized status items in themselves. These include two decorated styles named after findspots in the region (Ebbsfleet and Mortlake), as well as a style known as Grooved Ware, and the very fine Beaker pottery which may have been used at feasts for consuming alcoholic drinks.

These feasts were probably held on special occasions, perhaps festivals or marriages, when large quantities of food and drink (probably a kind of beer or mead) were consumed. Sometimes the remains of these feasts were carefully placed in pits, perhaps to give the gods their share, or to give back to the earth what was taken out of it. Groups of these pits, 4–5,000 years old, have been excavated by Museum of London archaeologists in west London, and were found to contain decorated pottery stacked up in piles, hazelnut shells, and bones of sheep or goat. Overall, excavations in the west London area have begun to produce a picture of what the landscape in Neolithic times would have looked like, and this area will probably produce some of the most valuable information in the future.

(*Top*) Pottery bowl. *Excavated at Heathrow in 1944, it is decorated in the 'Mortlake' style.*

(*Above*) Pottery beaker. *Found at Ham, possibly from a burial.*

Matters of Life and Death (2200–1200 BC)

5000	4000	3000	2000	1000	BC/AD

As population increased, the chalk hills and some of the areas of heavier soils were probably cleared of their dense forest cover and colonised. In such areas the pits and postholes of the earliest settlements first appear around 2000 BC. On the more easily cultivated areas, competition for land may have grown stronger. As a result, warfare may have increased and social divisions may have become greater.

As in the earlier periods, however, the places where people lived in this early part of the 'Bronze Age' are very difficult to find. Within the Greater London area, most sites are limited to isolated pits, which contain pottery, flints and occasionally loomweights, or quernstones for grinding grain. Sometimes the pits are clay-lined for storing grain or water. Examples of these settlement areas have been found on Hayes Common near Bromley and at

Female torso. *Found placed in the ditch of a Neolithic enclosure at Shepperton.*

(*Above*) Grooved Ware pottery. *These sherds (so named because of their grooved decoration) were found deliberately placed in pits near Harmondsworth.*

Bronze Age field. *The criss-cross pattern of dark lines show where an ard has scored the subsoil while preparing the ground for cultivation.*

Cooking pit. *From the same site in Bermondsey came a clay-lined cooking pit, dating to the Bronze Age or earlier. Water inside the pit would have been heated up by placing hot pebbles inside, and food cooked by boiling.*

Sipson in Hillingdon, where loomweights attest some of the earliest weaving known in London. The only clear settlement plan from the area dating to this period is from Thorpe in Surrey, where a fenced enclosure containing two round post-built houses with nearby pits and hearths was excavated in the 1970s. Evidently people at this time were still living in settled villages or small family groups, but as they did not dig deep postholes for their houses, the evidence has often been ploughed away in later times.

Sometimes it is possible to find traces of the fields which surrounded these settlements, in which crops were grown or animals grazed. At Hayes Common, and near Runnymede, large ditches have been found which probably acted both as property boundaries and as drainage ditches for the fields. Their existence is important because it adds weight to the suggestion that good land was becoming scarcer, and that those who had it had to mark out clearly what belonged to them. The concept of (non-portable) private property dates from at least this time, but the property need not have belonged just to an individual – it could have been controlled by a family or village.

Recently, direct evidence of farming in the period 2000–1000 BC was found during excavations in Bermondsey. As often happens, important prehistoric material was found accidentally while archaeologists were looking for something else: in this case they were trying to find a medieval riverbank. Underneath the river silts a buried Bronze Age field was found, with marks made by an ard, scored into the subsoil. These were produced when the undisturbed ground was first loosened using a 'rip-ard' dragged by a team of oxen, which gouged deep into the earth. After this, the soil was cultivated with hoes and spades (which also made marks in the subsoil). This is the earliest such evidence found so far in the lower Thames Valley.

A site on the south side of the former island of Bermondsey, also recently excavated, has given a glimpse of the other resources possibly used by people at this time. Trial excavations on a large former goods yard at Bricklayers Arms found that, at this period, there was a large lake to the south of the island which would have provided abundant fish and fowl. Right on the edge of the island, a layer of wood was found which may have been a place where boats were dragged ashore after fishing trips.

Due to the relative lack of settlement evidence, from around 2000 BC much of our knowledge of the London area comes from burials and religious offerings. The only definite prehistoric burial mound (or 'barrow) in the London area used to be in Teddington, and was excavated by a group of antiquarians in 1854. It was originally nearly 30 m across and 4 m high, and contained at least one central burial (probably a cremation) which yielded a bronze dagger and flints, and various other burials inserted into the mound at a later date. Unfortunately, only a few flints survive from this poorly-recorded excavation.

None of the other supposed burial mounds in the London area have been definitely proved to be of Bronze Age date. The only other one excavated, that on Parliament Hill on Hampstead Heath, contained nothing of prehistoric date and much material from recent centuries, suggesting it may have been used as a signalling beacon. However, a possible line of nine round barrows, long since ploughed out and covered by housing, has been identified on old aerial photographs taken around the Heathrow area. This raises the possibility that there were once many mounds which have been ploughed away over the centuries, leaving only their silted-up ditches to be spotted from the air.

Another reason for the lack of burial mounds may be that the main tradition in the period 2000–1000 BC was in fact to bury people in flat cremation

cemeteries, perhaps with small wooden markers above the graves. The remains of cemeteries have been found at various times in Acton, Kingsbury, Kingston, Littleton, Sunbury, Walton-on-Thames and Yiewsley. Most seem to have contained cremations with large urns inverted over them, and may represent the burials of extended family groups.

A more bizarre death was uncovered in 1987 by Museum of London archaeologists excavating in a gravel pit in Holloway Lane in Hillingdon. Cut into the overlying brickearth they found a large pit, over 2 m deep. Inside the pit they found the skeleton of a now-extinct wild cow, or aurochs. It had clearly been hunted and killed with at least six arrows, and then cut up. It was carefully arranged in the pit when the flesh was still on it, because the six flint arrowheads were found resting next to the bones. Some of the upper leg bones were missing, having possibly been carried away for food, while the horns may have been taken away as trophies. We know that the aurochs, a fierce, forest-dwelling animal much larger than the domestic cow, became extinct in Britain around 1300 BC, so we can perhaps imagine that at this time it was quite a rare and feared, or revered, animal. Certainly, the fact that it was carefully put into the pit and not eaten suggests that it was in some way special, and was perhaps a religious offering.

A further indication of the religious practices of people at this time is 'the Dagenham idol', a wooden figure dug out of the marshes in 1922. Previously thought to be Iron Age (700 BC – AD 43) it has recently been shown by radiocarbon dating to be as early as 2350–2140 BC.

Ploughing in the Bronze Age. *Reconstruction of cultivation next to the Thames based on recently excavated evidence from a site in Bermondsey.*

Cremation urns. *Found in once-extensive cemeteries to the west of London dating to 2000–1500 BC.*

Aurochs burial, *c.* 2000 BC. *The tail can be seen to the left, next to the jaw and the backbone, showing that the body was placed in the pit after being dismembered.*

Close-up of aurochs burial. *One of the six barbed and tanged arrowheads that killed the animal can be seen lying next to the bones where it was left inside the flesh.*

Towards the end of the third millennium BC, the very first metal objects were introduced into Britain, and a small number of copper axes and daggers have been found in the London area. Early copper items would have been prized as being scarce and valuable, and where supplies were not available, copies in flint and bone of copper daggers were made. Several have been found in the Thames. Although the ability to use metals was later to have very widespread effects, at first people's daily lives were unaffected by the discovery. For many centuries, the real centre of power in southern England had lain in the Wessex region and the upper Thames valley, demonstrated by the large-scale monuments, burial mounds and early metal supplies there. Just before 2000 BC, the addition of tin (about 10 per cent) to copper produced a new material, bronze, which was stronger than copper, easier to cast, and easy to recycle. Gradually, the importance of the Thames as a trade route for the distribution of copper and tin from its restricted sources in Ireland, Cornwall and Brittany grew, and societies in the lower Thames were able to take advantage of this. By about 1500 BC, the Wessex tradition was in decline, and the London region gradually became an important centre for both the production of metal objects and for controlling their trade. At the same time, the importance of metals in daily life slowly increased. Bronze axes and an increasing range of other bronze products began to be made as tools and as status symbols, just as copper objects had. In particular, much effort was put into making weapons of bronze, as if the display of power through the possession of weapons was becoming more important in society. A whole new range of products, such as spearheads, daggers, rapiers, and, later, swords and shields appear, suggesting new methods of fighting. This may have been because power was gradually becoming concentrated in the hands of smaller ruling elites who controlled access to fertile land and trade routes. At this period, and for many later centuries, we can imagine small chiefdoms in perpetual squabbles over access to land and trade routes, with the lives of the farming folk at the bottom of the scale being punctuated by raids and demands for new allegiances.

(*Right*) Bronze Age daggers. *The central copper dagger (with reconstructed handle) has been copied in bone and flint. All three were dredged from different stretches of the Thames.*

Hunting the aurochs. *Reconstruction based on recent excavations at Holloway Lane in Hillingdon. The hunters have flushed out the forest-dwelling aurochs into an ambush in the open.*

Axe–hammer and macehead, 2000–1200 BC. *Both would have been mounted on wooden shafts and were probably highly-prized objects as they are made of imported stone which has been carefully ground to the required shape.*

Heroes on Horseback (1200–700 BC)

5000	4000	3000	2000	1000	BC/AD

(*Above*) Middle Bronze Age metalwork. *The dagger (top left), spearhead (bottom left), razor (top right), axe (bottom right) and sword were all dredged from the Thames. They may have been thrown in as offerings to the gods.*

(*Right*) Land boundary. *One of a pair of ditches in Hillingdon dating to the Late Bronze Age.*

The general pattern of life established in the previous centuries continued, with greater agricultural production and trading advantages leading to denser settlement, increased population and greater wealth (at least for the ruling sections of society). From around 1200 BC there is a certain amount of evidence elsewhere for the gradual abandonment of the less favourable soils colonised a few centuries earlier. This was probably due to the combination of a worsening of the weather and an exhaustion of the soils through over-exploitation. This had the effect of increasing the number of people concentrated on the more fertile river valley areas, which made greater demands on the land. We see more field boundaries being dug to mark out the territory of particular groups, in places as far apart as Stanwell to the west of London and Upminster to the east. At Holloway Lane in Hillingdon, two parallel ditches have been traced for over 400 metres (1,300 ft). They may mark a droveway for herding cattle and sheep between settlements and pastures, or they may define an important hedge line.

The landscape by this time was relatively open, with most of the forest having been cleared for fields. At Runnymede, analysis of the remains of pollen, insects and snails in levels dating to between 950 BC and 650 BC has shown that there were damp grasslands for grazing cattle near the riverside, and fields of cereals on the drier ground of the slightly higher gravel terraces. Initially cattle provided the major source of meat, followed later on in the period by pigs. Dairy produce from cattle and sheep, such as milk and cheese, was also important, as were their hides and fleeces. From this period at least, the spinning and weaving of wool was a regular activity on every farm.

Fortified enclosure. *Reconstruction of the enclosure, dating to around 1000 BC, on the site of Queen Mary's Hospital in Carshalton. It overlooks the valley of the river Wandle which drains into the Thames (running across the centre of the picture).*

For the first time we can begin to see a variety of different settlement types across the landscape. The most common was still the small farming hamlet consisting of a cluster of circular post-built houses, probably thatched with straw, usually without any boundary fences. Examples of these have been excavated at Heathrow, and at Beddington in south London. One of the new kinds of site that developed at this time was the waterside settlement usually situated on a small island where a tributary meets the Thames. The most fully excavated example is at Runnymede, and there was almost certainly a similar site where the river Brent joins the Thames at Brentford. At Runnymede, the settlement had an enclosing double row of oak piles forming a frontage onto the Thames, where boats might have moored. This, together with its strategic position, and the presence of moulds and imported materials on site, suggests that the settlement played an important role in controlling the production and exchange of both local goods and footstuffs and exotic items along the river. Judging by items from Runnymede such as shale bracelets and bronze pins which were imported from outside the London area or even from the Continent, regular long-distance contacts were being made all along the Thames. As a result, the style of metal and pottery objects was noticeably influenced by continental fashions.

Such riverside sites may, however, have only been outposts for the much larger fortified settlements that also developed around 1000 BC. One of the earliest of these, roughly contemporary with Runnymede, is a 150 m (485 ft) diameter circular enclosure at Carshalton, strategically placed on the chalk Downs to look along the Wandle valley towards the Thames. The richness of the finds there, which include fine pottery, spindlewhorls, querns, some bronze metalworking debris, and an imported amber bead, together with its

Bronze Age settlement. *Excavation in progress on the Late Bronze Age levels at Runnymede.*

size and position, suggest that it was the main settlement of the area and the residence of the local ruler. It may have actually supported bronzesmiths carrying out metalworking with the raw materials passed on from traders on the Thames, and also acted as a regional place for meeting and bartering. Another, even larger, site has recently been identified by aerial photography at Mayfield Farm just to the south of Heathrow Airport, and 6.5 km away from Runnymede. It consists of two concentric ditches with a maximum diameter of 200 m enclosing an area of 3.14 hectares (7.75 acres), and trial trenches cut into it reveal its date as some time in the Late Bronze Age (1200–700 BC). It is the largest such enclosure of this period in the lower Thames valley, and if it is fully excavated it may prove to have been a very important regional centre which controlled a large territory.

Another reason for the building of large defended settlements in this period may have been the increased threat of warfare due to higher population and greater competition for land. Over the previous centuries, it seems as if power was gradually being concentrated into the hands of an ever-smaller number of local rulers, who attempted to hold on to their power by force, or threat of force, and by protecting what they had by building boundaries and strongholds. As pressure on the land grew, fortifications increased and a sort of warrior aristocracy seems to have developed all over Europe. Their 'heroic' lifestyle of feasting and fighting was later immortalised in Celtic legends, and seems to have persisted for over 1,000 years.

Double-ditched enclosure. *Aerial photograph of a large site just to the south of Heathrow Airport recently shown by small-scale excavations to be of Late Bronze Age date (1200–700 BC).*

One of the important new developments was horse-riding, which may have transformed fighting techniques. A ruler could now have a small band of riders at his or her disposal, ready to respond quickly to any threat or engage in cattle raids into rivals' territory. Slashing swords rather than thrusting rapiers reflected this change from foot to horse-borne combat. Excavations at Runnymede have shown that antler 'cheek pieces' for reins were manufactured on site. Horses were also used as a means of displaying wealth and power, and a range of trappings such as decorative bronze discs were made at this time.

Other items produced more for display than use include bronze shields, shown in experiments to be far less effective than wooden or leather ones, and huge barbed spearheads that were probably too heavy for use in battle, and may have been for ceremonial use. Nevertheless, the bulk of the weapons produced were very effective spears, swords and axes.

The Late Bronze Age was also characterised by a great increase in bronze manufacturing, such that it came to be used for everyday items such as chisels, hammers, pins and razors. Some of these items, particularly the smaller ones, have been excavated from settlement sites where they were clearly accidentally lost or thrown away, but the majority of metalwork has been found in places where it was probably deliberately deposited. Metalwork had been buried in earlier periods too, but in this period there is a spread all along the lower Thames valley of hoards of metalwork buried deliberately, which usually consist of fragments of swords, axes, spears, tools and lumps of copper ingot. There is probably no single explanation for all of these hoards: they may have been buried for safekeeping by bronzesmiths prior to melting down for scrap, or they may be offerings. The other major source of bronze finds has been the

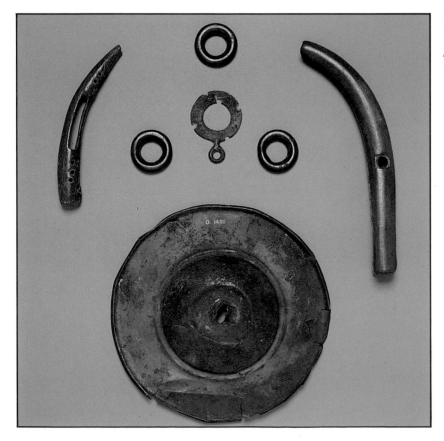

Horse equipment. *Comprising two antler 'cheek pieces', three bronze rings, a bronze pendant and a 'phalera' which was probably a decorative disc.*

Bronze tools. *Shown here are a knife, a gouge, a chisel and a sickle, all with modern hafts.*

(*Below*) Hoard of metalwork, 900–600 BC. *The hoard was recovered from the terminal of a ditch on a site at Egham in Surrey. The 78 pieces were deliberately deposited in two separate groups, possibly inside bags which have since perished.*

River Thames, from which hundreds of items have been dredged, mainly in the nineteenth century. These tend to be large, complete objects such as swords, and may well form part of the long-lived tradition of ritual river deposits noted from previous centuries.

This theory gains strength from the fact that, apart from a probable small burial mound excavated recently on the Thames bank at Southwark, no formal burial from this period has been found. One theory is that the dead were cremated and their ashes scattered, or they were placed on platforms until the flesh decayed or was eaten by scavengers, and the bones were then scattered. This may explain the presence of human bones in pits or in settlement refuse at this time, and it is probably significant that some of the many skulls dredged from the Thames have been dated to this period by the radiocarbon method. Higher ranking individuals may have had their weapons deposited in the Thames to accompany them into the afterlife. Other finds may represent offerings made directly to the gods, or may even be the result of casual losses from boats over a long period.

In terms of the density and range of settlements, and the strong evidence of wealth and power, the period 1200–700 BC may have represented a high point in the fortunes of the London area before the Roman invasion.

Axe and haft. *This socketed axe, nearly 3000 years old, was found in a silted-up river channel near Shepperton, complete with its original two-piece wooden haft.*

Cargo on the Thames. *A reconstruction of a Bronze Age boat transferring cargo and passengers from one side of the river to the other.*

(*Left*) A warrior's funeral. *Reconstruction showing how some of the Bronze Age metalwork from the Thames may have been deposited there. Here the funeral pyre is being ignited and the warrior's sword is being offered to the river.*

Hillforts and Farmsteads (700–200 BC)

| 5000 | 4000 | 3000 | 2000 | 1000 | BC/AD |

Over a short period of time, the population of the London area could rise and fall depending on whether the crop yields were good, and whether there were epidemics or conflicts. Over the course of the last millennium BC, however, the general trend was one of continued increase, aided by an apparent improvement in the climate between about 600 and 300 BC, which increased crop yields and allowed the recolonisation of marginal lands.

The tradition of defended hill-top settlements continued with the building of an enclosure on Wimbledon Common around 700 BC. This consisted of a single bank and a 4 m deep, 10 m wide, ditch enclosing an area of about 4.75 hectares (12 acres). Unlike central southern England, the London region has relatively few of these hillforts. Most of the recognisable ones are just outside the area on the hills to the north and south of the valley, and are not very securely dated. Some, such as St Ann's Hill near Chertsey, have evidence of occupation as early as about 750 BC, while others such as Caesar's Camp, Keston, or the adjacent enclosures of Loughton Camp and Ambresbury Banks in Epping Forest may have been built several centuries later.

No excavations have been carried out in the interior of these hilltop settlements, so we have no clear idea of their role in the area. However, by comparing them with other enclosures excavated elsewhere, it is possible to suggest that they combined the roles of storehouse, market, noble's residence, industrial centre and citadel. With power still concentrated in the hands of a small number of dynasties, the defended enclosure would have been the outward expression of the ruler's power. The maintenance of this power depended on family ties and the loyalty or obedience of subjects, and one way in which these were kept up was by providing work and protection in return for tributes of produce. Thus, in return for being able to farm the land, subjects may have had to give a certain percentage of their crops, meat, hides or wool to their ruler. One probable role of the hillfort was to store this grain to feed the ruler's household, which might have included specialist craftworkers and warriors, and to exchange products such as wool for other commodities. The hillforts may also have included areas where cattle could be enclosed and even where crops could be grown, and they provided a refuge for the surrounding population in times of crisis. It is also worthwhile noting that the force which could be used against outside threats could also be used to keep subjects under control: the protection of a ruler would have been (literally) a double-edged sword.

The backbone of the economy remained farming, and the vast majority of the population lived in small farmsteads supporting an extended family. Although they are much less easy to discover than hillforts, remains of several of these farms have been found in the London area. The few pits and gullies found undisturbed in areas of Central London by the Houses of Parliament, in Leicester Square and in Southwark, are probably the scanty remains of

(*Above*) Hillfort. *The aerial photograph clearly shows the ditch and rampart of the hillfort on Wimbledon Common, which dates to around 700 BC.*

(*Below*) Iron Age settlement, *c.* 400–150 BC. *A reconstruction based on excavations at Dawley in west London which revealed three houses, a smaller hut for storage or cooking, and a number of small granaries.*

such hamlets. Better-preserved and more extensive remains have been found in less built-up areas further west and east. From around 700 BC, a number of new settlements seem to have been founded. Most of these 'Early Iron Age' sites, such as that revealed during excavations at Heathrow Airport in 1969, consist only of a few pits, probably used first for storing grain and then dumping rubbish, as the standing buildings have not survived. A clearer picture of the lifestyle of these farming communities is given by looking at the excavations of slightly later settlements dating to between 400 and 100 BC.

Sites at Rainham in the borough of Havering to the east and at Dawley and Bedfont to the west, have produced evidence of circular houses, granaries, storage pits and field ditches. At Dawley, excavations by the Museum of London revealed four circular houses between 6 and 12 m (20 − 40 ft) in diameter. Like most houses of this period, they are recognisable by the ring-shaped ditches which formed either the bedding trench for the walls or the gulley to catch the rainwater dripping from the eaves of the thatched roof. They would have had a hearth in the middle for warmth and cooking, and smoke would have escaped from a hole in the top of the roof. Internal partitions may have divided the houses into sleeping and living areas, while a smaller hut nearby might have served for storage. In addition to the houses, at least ten 'four-post structures' were found. These are usually interpreted as granaries raised on stilts to protect the grain from damp and vermin, a theory supported by the presence of grain in one of the postholes.

Dagger and scabbard. *This iron dagger has a sheath made of bronze bands, with a wooden lining. It was found in the Thames, probably at Mortlake, and is dated to 550–450 BC.*

(*Right*) An Iron Age house. *Excavation in progress at Dawley on a house with foundation trench and internal posts. A much smaller hut is in the foreground.*

The hamlet was probably lived in by one or two families over several generations, raising sheep and cattle for meat, milk, hides and wool, and growing crops such as barley and wheat. Clay loomweights and a spindle whorl suggest that weaving continued to be practised, and metal slag may indicate that even small-scale ironworking was carried out.

Another site at Heathrow, excavated in advance of airport construction in 1944, revealed up to 11 houses (although not all were occupied at the same time). Most interestingly, the southern part of the site contained a square building interpreted as a temple. It is not securely dated, but contained sherds of pottery similar to those found in the huts, and is also paralleled by structures of similar date in the hillfort at Danebury in Hampshire. Neither site has provided direct evidence that the buildings were used for religious rites, but similar structures abroad definitely seem to have been temples. If this is so, then Heathrow provides very early evidence for rituals being carried out in a formal building rather than in natural places such as forest groves.

The only other direct evidence for religious rites at this period is the continued deposition of fine metalwork in the Thames, such as a series of daggers and sheaths dating to between 600 and 300 BC, and a unique shield, dated by radiocarbon to about 350 BC, discovered in a silted-up river channel near Chertsey. There were still no formal burials, and we can only guess at how the dead were treated.

The Thames, in the early part of this period, was still an important trade route linking ultimately with the Rhine and the powerful chieftains in Germany. The effect of this trade is seen both in imports such as a stone battleaxe found in the Thames near Brentford, and in continental influences on the styles of daggers. In the third and second centuries BC, trade may have shifted more to southern Britain, most notably through the port at Hengistbury Head in Dorset, which received imports of wine and pottery from France. This may have led to a temporary decline in the fortunes of the Thames traders, who were already suffering from the fall-off of the bronze trade, lasting until the revival of extensive trade with the Rhineland from around 100 BC.

One of the most significant changes occurring in this period was the development of ironworking, which was first introduced into the London area around 650 BC. Although at first the products were not much better than bronze ones, the introduction gradually had widespread social effects.

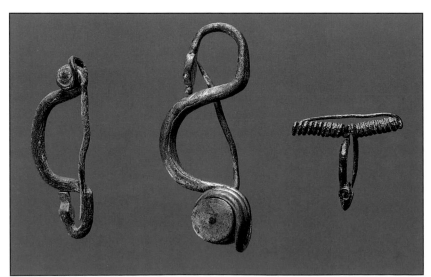

(*Left*) Brooches. *Three brooches for fastening cloaks at the neck, all found on the foreshore of the Thames.*

(*Above*) The Chertsey shield. *A unique shield of the Middle Iron Age, belonging to an individual of high rank.*

(*Right*) Iron sword. *Dug out of a former river channel during gravel extraction near Chertsey.*

As iron ores are much more abundant than copper and tin, it was no longer necessary to rely on long-distance exchange networks to obtain metal. By about 550 BC, iron from relatively local sources was being regularly used for making tools and weapons all over southern Britain. As a result the dynasties of the Lower Thames valley, which had previously controlled the production and distribution of bronze, lost their dominant position and found themselves on a more equal footing with communities from other areas. A few communities clearly benefited from the move to ironworking, as they were well-placed to exploit the sources of iron in the Weald lands of Surrey and Sussex. Away from the Weald, just outside London at Brooklands, Weybridge, excavations in the 1960s and 70s produced good evidence for ironworking. In one area, six smelting furnaces were found and in another were found features probably associated with the production of artefacts. Just one kilometre away from the site, on the slopes of St George's Hill (the site of an undated hillfort), is an outcrop of iron carbonates which probably provided the raw material for the smelting. The hillfort may possibly have controlled a trade in iron products, though without excavation this cannot be proved. Finds of iron slag on smaller sites such as Dawley suggest that some ironworking, perhaps for simple tools, may have been quite a local affair, while more complex items such as swords would have been produced by specialist craftworkers. The bronze industry did not disappear. Although the quantity of items decreased, their quality increased as master specialists began to produce elaborate prestige items such as shields, dagger fittings, horse decorations and brooches for fastening cloaks and jerkins.

Heathrow temple and village, *c.* 200 BC. *The temple may have had a colonnade rather than walls, giving open access to the interior, which probably contained idols and offerings left by worshippers.*

The Approach of Rome (200 BC–AD 43)

From around 300 BC the small rustic republic of Rome began to enlarge its territory to such an extent that by 120 BC it controlled the whole of Italy and had begun its encirclement of the Mediterranean. Gradually the areas north of the Alps began supplying the empire with raw materials, food and people, in the form both of slaves and mercenary soldiers. In exchange the leaders of these Celtic-speaking societies received political guarantees and luxury goods such as wine which stimulated their desire for the trappings of Mediterranean civilisation. Where the goods themselves could not be obtained, local copies were made.

One of the first Mediterranean traditions to be copied was coinage. Celtic-style coinage was widely produced in Gaul (now France) and first appeared in Britain perhaps before 200 BC, in the form of imported gold coins. These may have been brought back by returning mercenaries, or by immigrant leaders from Gaul and Belgica, or may have been given as gifts to local leaders. The use of gold and silver coinage was soon established amongst the upper classes of society for social payments such as dowries for brides. Iron bars of regular shape, known as 'currency bars' may also have been traded as standard units, which could then be directly made into tools or weapons.

A second type of lower level coinage was introduced some time after 100 BC, where it is known especially from six large hoards in west London. It is made of a tin-rich bronze known as 'potin' and was probably used for more direct transactions, particularly at markets at tribal boundaries. The dense distribution of potin coins around London suggests the area was of some importance at this time, though little settlement evidence has yet been found.

Potin coins have been discovered on a huge but little-known site in London which may possibly have acted as one of these markets. It is known as Uphall Camp and occupies 19.4 hectares (48 acres) on the River Roding in Ilford.

(*Right*) Uphall Camp, *c.* 100 BC. *The outline of the settlement is known from old maps and some of the internal layout from excavations. It is not yet known how densely occupied the site was in the Iron Age. Its position right by the river Roding suggests that river-borne trade may have been an important part of the settlement's economy.*

(*Right below*) Excavating Uphall. *The photograph shows the outline of a large round house with a porch which would probably have been occupied by a family.*

Iron Age coins. *In the top row is a gold stater of the mid first century BC, a silver coin of the Iceni, dating to around AD 40, and a bronze coin of Cunobelin, king of the Catuvellauni, of about the same date. The lower group of coins are part of a hoard of 365 coins of a tin-rich bronze found near Shepperton.*

This makes it almost as large as the famous hillfort of Maiden Castle in Dorset, but it has been invisible for years beneath houses and a chemical works. Excavations in the 1980s by the Passmore Edwards Museum on a small portion of the site have revealed at least eight round houses, some rectangular structures, numerous granaries, a possible internal road, and traces of ironworking.

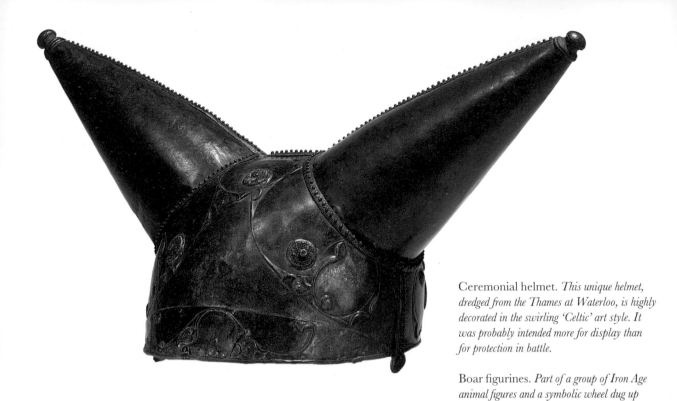

Ceremonial helmet. *This unique helmet, dredged from the Thames at Waterloo, is highly decorated in the swirling 'Celtic' art style. It was probably intended more for display than for protection in battle.*

Boar figurines. *Part of a group of Iron Age animal figures and a symbolic wheel dug up on Hounslow Heath last century.*

Horse and chariot equipment. *Above the horse bit is a decorated 'horn cap' which may have been attached to the hub of a chariot or to the yoke as grips for the driver's hand. Below is a 'terret' through which the horses' reins were passed.*

Tankard. *This large vessel, with a capacity of about four pints, is made of oak staves covered in bronze. It would probably have been used for communal drinking at feasts. Found in the Thames at Brentford.*

Although no identifiable continental imports have been found, the settlement may have acted as a local trading centre, before its apparent abandonment perhaps some time around 60 BC.

The full impact of Mediterranean expansion was not felt until 55 BC. As the small chieftains of the London area were engaging in sporadic cattle-raiding and warfare amongst themselves, the Roman Empire was still expanding. In 62 BC the chance of glory, and pressure from merchants to expand the markets of the Empire, prompted the general Pompey to annexe Syria and Crete and shortly after this in 59 BC his rival Julius Caesar began the conquest of Gaul, which took two years. A year later Brittany rebelled against Roman rule and received help from Britain. After putting down the rebellion, Caesar decided to invade Britain as a punishment and to assess the potential of its resources for the Empire. We now enter the era of written history, as the main source for this episode is the account of it written by Caesar himself in his book *Gallic Wars*. As well as describing his campaigns in Gaul and Britain, Caesar also describes the customs of the inhabitants he meets. It provides vital information on how society was organised in Britain at this time, although it has to be realized that Caesar was only providing one side of the story, and was writing in order to increase his prestige in Rome.

In August 55 BC his army of 10,000 set sail from Boulogne, landing on the south coast near Deal. After a battle on the beach, the British leaders asked for peace, but a severe storm damaged Caesar's fleet. After these had been repaired, the Roman force returned to France, determined to invade again the next year.

In July 54 BC a much larger force set sail, consisting of 25,000 infantry and 2,000 cavalry, together with baggage and supplies in over 800 ships. Again the landing was successful and the force advanced and captured a hillfort to which the British had retired (probably Bigberry near Canterbury). Again, however, a storm wrecked the fleet and in the delay while repairs were effected the British tribes chose a single war leader, Cassivellaunus, who ruled a territory north of the Thames. Caesar eventually advanced towards this territory, having to fight a battle to cross the Thames, somewhere in the London area. He describes the battle in his *Gallic Wars* thus:

> When I discovered what the enemy's plans were, I led the army to the river Thames and the territory of Cassivellaunus. There is only one place where the river can be forded, and even there with difficulty. When we reached it, I noticed large enemy forces drawn up on the opposite bank. The bank had also been fortified with sharp stakes fixed along it, and, as I discovered from prisoners and deserters, similar stakes had been driven into the river bed and were concealed beneath the water.

> I immediately gave orders for the cavalry to go ahead and the legions to follow them. As the infantry crossed, only their heads were above the water, but they pressed on with such speed and determination that both infantry and cavalry were able to attack together. The enemy, unable to stand up to this combined force, abandoned the river bank and took to flight.

Cassivellaunus returned to his stronghold in the wooded area north of the Thames, possibly at Wheathampstead in Hertfordshire, and other tribes surrendered and revealed its location. Caesar then attacked and gained the surrender of the British leader. Peace was gained in exchange for hostages and annual

Battle across the Thames. *Caesar's invading army clashing with native warriors on the north bank of the river in 54 BC.*

Wheel-turned pottery. *Two bowls from a site at Crayford, dating to the early 1st century AD.*

Excavations at Rainham. *A line of loomweights show where an upright loom was abandoned inside a Late Iron Age triple-ditched enclosure.*

tribute to Rome, and Caesar set sail for home. Although Roman soldiers were not to return for almost a hundred years, after Caesar's invasions the links with Rome had been forged and Britain was never to be the same again.

One of the major consequences of the invasions seems to have been the formation of large political units often called tribes, but perhaps better described as small states. Certain dynasties and chiefdoms had already joined together to fight Caesar, but in the face of the Empire just across the Channel, these units seem to have become permanent, rather in the way in which the Zulu nation emerged in the nineteenth century in South Africa as a response to the British Empire. With the development of coinage, many leaders struck their own coins, which approximately map out their territories. One crucial fact to emerge is that, at least in the hundred years before AD 43, the Thames seems to have been used as a boundary, with the Catuvellauni and the Trinovantes to the north, and the Atrebates and the Cantii to the south. These political units had their centres well away from the Thames in places such as St Albans, Colchester and Canterbury, with the result that the London area no longer held the central importance it once had. At least, there is no evidence of large central settlements: most occupation sites seem to have been small farms which continued on into the Roman period, seemingly little affected by the political changes going on around them. Examples of such settlements have been excavated at Beddington and Sanderstead in south London, and at Rainham and Crayford in east London. Typically they consist of the same cluster of round houses and granaries that we have seen already, where the traditional mixed economy was practised. An important development in this period is the mould-board plough with an iron share, which enabled the heavier clay soils to be cultivated, and allowed the population to increase. Around the time of the Roman invasion, it has been estimated that population levels in the Thames valley were as high as they were in rural areas in the early medieval period.

Central London around 30 BC, looking south-west. *The river is much wider than it is today, with extensive areas of mudflats. The areas of modern Bermondsey, Southwark and Westminster are gravel islands. Rivers now channelled underground, such as the Fleet (bottom right) can clearly be seen.*

Thus, although the fertile areas of the Thames valley were being heavily exploited for the production of grain, vegetables, milk, meat, wool and leather, central trading and distribution seem to have shifted to the emergent towns or 'oppida' to the north and south. These maintained ever-closer contacts with the continent in the form of trade, especially of luxury imports for the elite. We see the introduction into south-eastern England of wheel-made pottery and its local copies, and of wine drinking. The distinctive Celtic art style also flowered at this time as a result of Mediterranean contact. In return the British leaders supplied corn, cattle, gold, silver, hides, slaves and hunting dogs.

The Thames was still an important focus for ritual activity, as is shown by the metalwork deposited in it. Although it has been found in a smaller quantity, it consists of unique and very elaborate items such as the shield from Battersea and the helmet from Waterloo. These may have been offerings made by the very highest tribal leaders, and, together with the accounts of Classical writers, they can provide us with a picture of the lifestyle of the elite of these Celtic-speaking groups.

By the time of Caesar's invasions, society in southern Britain was highly stratified. At the lowest level were slaves who had been bought or captured to work on the land. Above them were the mass of the people, who are best described as tenant farmers, unfree and landless. Above them, according to writers, were the elite, who were themselves divided into two basic groups. The first were the knights ('*equites*'), so-called because horse-riding was an indication of rank, and the second were the members of the learned class which included druids, bards and seers. The elite continued to aspire to the

The Battersea shield. *This magnificent example of Iron Age decorative art is made of bronze sheets and panels covering a core of wood or leather. The roundels are inlaid with coloured glass.*

Offering the shield to the river. *The reconstruction brings to life the possibility that the shield might have been offered to the river at the time of the Roman invasion to ask the gods for help in a time of crisis.*

heroic lifestyle of feasting, boasting and fighting which had characterised their ancestors. Of fundamental concern were prestige and respect, such that an individual's appearance of wealth and power was as important as possessing it. Being able to wear fine jewellery and armour, or offer them into the river, was just one way of indicating high rank. Chariots had been added decades before to the warrior's fighting techniques, and these, together with the horses, would have been finely ornamented. One of the mysteries of London archaeology is why this finery continues to be deposited in the river when all the large settlements are apparently much further inland. Were the elite of these societies journeying to the Thames to perform rituals to emphasise their differences from the tribes on the other side of the river, or do important riverside settlements, such as trading ports, remain to be discovered?

The end of the era began when the powerful Catuvellaunian leader Cunobelin, perhaps the grandson of Cassivellaunus, died in AD 40. He was succeeded by his anti-Roman sons, Togodubnus and Caratacus, who pursued a vigorous policy of expansion by annexing the territories of nearby smaller tribes. Following the annexation of his kingdom, Verica, leader of the Atrebates, fled to Rome to ask for help. At the time, the new emperor Claudius was looking to improve his popularity with the army and senate, and the anti-Roman policies of Togodubnus and Caratacus were an ideal excuse to mount an invasion. The Roman army landed in Kent and overcame the British forces, in the spring of AD 43, a date which marks the beginning of nearly 400 years of occupation, and the conventional end of prehistory.

Bronze coins of Cunobelin and of the Emperor Claudius. *Cunobelin's death disrupted the balance of power in southern England and, after three years of unrest, provided a justification for Claudius to mount an invasion.*